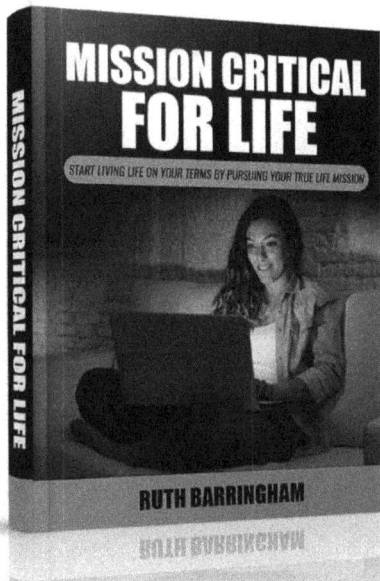

MISSION CRITICAL FOR LIFE

FOR LIFE

START LIVING LIFE ON YOUR TERMS BY PURSUING YOUR TRUE LIFE MISSION

RUTH BARRINGHAM

Mission Critical For Life:

Start Living Your Life on Your Terms by Pursuing Your True Life Mission

By

Ruth Barringham

Copyright

Due Diligence

When it comes to making decisions, especially those based on ideas from reading this book, you are advised to do your own due diligence and use caution and seek advice from a qualified professional before taking any action.

The author nor the publisher of this book assume any responsibility whatsoever for any losses or damages incurred from any actions taken from reading this book.

This book is only meant as a general educational information product and in no way should be regarded as a substitute for professional advice.

Further, the author and the publisher do not warrant any actions taken as a result of using the material contained in this book and are not liable for any damages including injury and legal costs.

The author and the publisher do, however, wish the very best to all who improve their lives and financial situation due the improvements gained from using the material discussed in this book.

Find more inspirational books at:

https://cheritonhousepublishing.com

Disclaimer

Although the publisher and the author have made every effort to ensure that the information in this book was correct at press time and while this publication is designed to provide accurate information in regard to the subject matter covered, the publisher and the author assume no responsibility for errors, inaccuracies, omissions, or any other inconsistencies herein and hereby disclaim any liability to any party for any loss, damage, or disruption caused by errors or omissions, whether such errors or omissions result from negligence, accident, or any other cause.

The information provided in this book is for informational purposes only and is not intended to be a source of advice or credit analysis with respect to the material presented. The information and/or documents contained in this book do not constitute legal or financial advice and should never be used without first consulting with a financial professional to determine what may be best for your individual needs.

The publisher and the author do not make any guarantee or other promise as to any results that may be obtained from using the content of this book. You should never make any investment decision without first consulting with your own financial advisor and conducting your own research and due diligence. To the maximum extent permitted by law, the publisher and the author disclaim any and all liability in the event any information, commentary, analysis, opinions, advice and/or recommendations contained in this book prove to be inaccurate, incomplete or unreliable, or result in any investment or other losses.

Table Of Contents

Introduction

10 Steps to Your Life Mission

"You're not born this way, you get this way." ~ Seth Godin

During the creation of this book I was looking online at other books about having and pursuing a true life mission. And what I discovered was that nearly all of them were about pursuing a religious mission.

But that is not what this book is about.

This book is for anyone who is tired of living life on other people's terms and wants to find and work on their own life mission.

According to the dictionary, a mission is "an important assignment carried out for political, religious or commercial purposes. A long term assignment."

And according to the thesaurus, it means, a vocation, calling, function, pursuit or aim.

So what does all this mean?

What Exactly is a Mission?

In this book, when we talk about having a mission, it means doing something that you really want to do.

It's not what you think you 'should' do, or what you think would be best to do, or what you think would help others.

No. Your mission is something that you want to do that gets you excited just thinking about it. It's something. You want to do every day. Something you enjoy.

I've read many books and articles about how people get ill, and even die from diseases like cancer, because of not being able to pursue their true life's mission.

This can be seen clearly in cases where patients have been told that they're dying and only have a few weeks/months to live. So they quit their jobs and spend what little time they have left doing what they really want to do which may be travelling or art or writing or spending time in nature or helping their favourite charity.

And pursuing their true life mission in this way literally saves their lives, because making their mission their priority removes the usual stresses from life and so the disease leaves their body. And if you find that hard to believe a quick Google search will prove it's true in many cases.

There are also places like the Kushi Institute in America that helped people cure cancer through macrobiotic diet. But that's a whole other subject. And sadly, the Kushi Institute has now closed down due to the deaths of the two owners and founders.

When choosing your own mission, as well as it being something you want to do more than anything else, it also needs to be something you can do for the rest of your life.

And don't make the mistake of thinking that spending time doing something that is only for you is selfish. It's not.

When you're content, it has a positive knock-on effect to the rest of your life, and to those around you too.

When you know that no matter how stressful and difficult the rest of your life can be, you can always go home, lock the door, and work on your mission, because your mission will always be there for you.

You'll no longer 'need' the company of others all the time. You won't' feel compelled, or want to, hang around with others or spend time socialising just to fill your days.

Always having your mission to turn to means you'll have the confidence to walk away from any person or situation you don't want to be part of.

You're also going to discover how having a mission will earn you respect from others that you never had before.

And your mission can be anything you want it to be. It can be financial, creative, skillful or even religious.

No one can choose your mission for you. It is completely your decision. And later, we'll look at how to choose your mission.

But for now, what I really need to impress upon you is how much better your life will be when you have your mission.

You'll need (and want) to purse your mission ruthlessly and without apology. And it will change your life in ways you cannot imagine.

In time, you'll benefit financially, and it will improve your relationships with others, because you won't be as needy for their company anymore, so you'll become more attractive to them once you start disappearing from your social circle more to work on your mission.

The most surprising thing of all is that it will make you feel powerful. You'll finally be the dictator of your own life when you start saying no to the demands of others. You'll no longer be at their beck and call which will also make them more respectful of you.

And it all begins with finding your mission and dedicating your life to it.

And this is what we'll be looking at first. Finding your exact mission. And you'll know it when you find it because it will light your fire so that you can't wait to get up every day to work on it.

This book is your manual on how to discover what you want to do and how to be the best at what you do.

But it's not just about what you do, but how you are. More specifically who you need to become so that you can have the confidence to go after what you want without apology.

And it starts with your attitude, which means you have to stop being grateful for what little life throws you, and get out and see the endless possibilities waiting for you. But that will only happen if you have the guts to stop being a sheep, break away from the flock, and have the guts to go after what you want.

It's time to stop letting others walk all over you. And you do this by not allowing people to look down on you.

You're about to learn 10 things that can change your life today.

You're going to go from socially awkward to extremely confident and get respect from those around you.

And it's not just respect. You'll also gain money, influence and peace of mind.

If you don't have those things now, it's because you're needy; needy of other people's attention, needy of being 'liked' and needy of thinking that others can't live without you.

You have to stop letting neediness ruin your life. What makes you needy is not having a mission. But once you do, you can prioritise it, which means embracing your darker side so that you can say 'no' to others more often.

You see, in order to pursue your mission, you're going to have to be merciless and let go of the things that no longer serve you, which can be hard to do.

To let go you need to understand that everything in life is made up of Yin and Yang, which means we can't have one thing without the other, like without rain there are no flowers.

And so it is with us. Just like you can't have light without it casting a shadow. We think we are 'nice' (light) but we also have a dark side. Our darker side is our shadow and sometimes our shadow needs to be seen so that we can say no to people.

Don't get me wrong though. I'm not saying you should behave badly. Only that in order to have wholeness, you need balance in your life which means having both light and shadow.

So stop hiding your shadow and let it be seen. Have the confidence and self-respect to say 'no' to people if you don't want to do something.

But before we continue, here are some words of caution:

Just as a surgeon's knife can be used to save a life or end a life, so you need to take care with your own words and actions.

Always remember to use wisdom and ethics when applying what you read in this book, otherwise you may end up hurting someone or getting yourself into trouble. Or both.

But wisely using what you're about to learn, will lead you to creating your dream job and living your dream life, with your life mission critical.

Chapter 1

Prioritise Your Mission

I read a lot of self help books, partly because I can always use some help, and partly because the subject of psychology fascinates me. The more I read, the more I realise how powerful our minds are.

There's a saying that whether you say you can or you say you can't, you're right. That's because it's not so much what we can or can't do, but whether we believe we can do something or not.

Another way of expressing it, is Self Image. We all have our own self image and we are quick to use negative terms about ourselves, such as loser, failure, stupid, etc.

When we do this we are our own worst critic and this is what holds us back. Just our own negative self-talk.

But have you ever seen the self-image of successful and highly motivated people? They ooze confidence and self-esteem with the most important trait being self-esteem, and it's self-esteem that gives a person confidence and self-assurance in a way that cannot even be imagined until you try it. Until you act with self-esteem.

So what you have to do is emulate people with self-esteem.

Going back to the dictionary, the word self-esteem means, "confidence in one's own worth or abilities. Self-respect."

Now pay particular attention to the word 'self-respect' in the definition of the word self-esteem because among other things it means, 'a feeling that one is behaving with honour and dignity.' And that's important. It's so important that I'll say it again. Self-respect is 'a feeling that one is behaving with honour and dignity.'

Now let me ask you a question. Do you feel like you act with honour and dignity in everything you say and do? If not, then doing so will give you the self-respect you need.

You can't feel good about yourself or about what you're doing if you know you're a cheat, a liar, dishonest, rude or nasty. Behaving with dignity and self-respect will automatically give you self-confidence and self-assurance which leads full circle back to self-esteem.

This means that if you're behaving badly, it has to stop or you'll never have self-esteem or self-respect, which, in real terms, means you must start exercising a change in attitude towards yourself.

It's just like in the opening quote of this chapter, by Seth Godin, "You're not born this way, you get this way." This is why people with self-esteem 'exercise' (act) this way, so that they become (get) this way.

Once again it all comes down to mindset and the self-image that you hold of yourself. In fact there's a whole book on the importance of self-image call 'Psycho-Cybernetics" by Dr Maxwell

Maltz and it's a fascinating book that I've read several times, and it says that until you change your self-image, nothing in your life will change or improve.

You can only gain confidence and self-esteem in your mind. It starts when you decide to stop accepting the crumbs thrown to you by others and turn your attitude around 180 degrees.

Stand with a straight back and strong chest and realise that you have no peers because you're far more advanced/superior to everyone else.

Once you accept this, your new superior confidence will grow quickly and make you more persuasive and give you self-esteem and your every word will radiate with confidence. You'll quickly realise that this is the secret to living life on your terms.

People will always treat you as badly as you allow them to, so stop giving them permission and see how it dramatically changes your life.

And don't use the excuse that you can't get whatever you want because you look ordinary or because you think you're ugly. With self-esteem you can yield power, money, respect, influence, opportunity, and you'll exude a compelling attractiveness that can inspire devotion in others.

If you think it's not true, try it.

You'll quickly discover that once you exercise self-esteem, you can easily get anything you want. It can help you get jobs, promotions, dates, and money.

People will want to buy from you and socialise with you and it will become easy to persuade others to do things for you, and respect your boundaries

But don't get me wrong. I'm not saying you should start acting like a bully or shirking your responsibilities in life. I'm simply saying that by following the advice in this book you can turn your life around and go from being a needy push-over to a strong person full of self-esteem and dignity who knows what they want and how to get it.

And it all stars with the following 10 simple steps that you can start implementing today.

How to Gain Self-esteem

10 Secrets to make part of your everyday life

1. Prioritise your mission
2. Stop being needy
3. Don't give away all your time and money
4. Financially secure your future
5. You have no peers
6. Remember that nice guys always finish last
7. Time is your time all the time
8. Ignore the masses
9. Have patience
10. Persistence

1. Prioritise Your Mission

This is the most important of all these 10 steps because having a mission really is THAT important and it will stop you being needy.

Most people spend their lives being needy. Some even waste their lives being needy for things as worthless as getting Facebook 'Likes.'

So what makes people needy?

Not having a mission.

Anyone who has a mission and pursues it relentlessly is never needy of anything or anyone, and it transforms their life in ways they could never imagine.

Take for example a woman I knew. She used to dress like a slob in clothes that weren't even fit to be given to the charity store. Her house was always a mess, she ate badly, was overweight and did nothing all day.

Then she met a self-made wealthy woman and felt inspired to do the same.

She cleaned up her house and herself, got a job, saved all her money, bought a car, and disappeared from her usual social circle to spend time planning and building her own business.

I lost touch with her eventually because she was so busy, so wealthy, had slimmed down, moved away and had a whole new circle of friends and business associates. She also became the most confident and hard-working person I'd ever known.

How did she do it all?

She decided to get a mission. She wanted to build her own business and live an enviable lifestyle.

Every day she poured her heart and soul into her mission and turned her life completely around. The result was the biggest and most amazing life-transformation I've ever seen.

Your own mission doesn't have to be money-orientated. It can be anything you want.

But as you can see from my friend's experience, not only did her mission make her rich, but it improved everything about her. She transformed her home, her body, her mind, her relationships, her wealth and her whole life.

Having a mission enabled her to walk away from her old life without looking back and without apologising to anyone.

Gandhi is another example of how powerful having a mission can be. He also transformed his life when he set out on his mission to take back India from British rule. His mission was never about money yet he too poured his heart and soul into it and changed his life, and the life of all Indians, in a different way to my rich friend.

Abraham Lincoln is another great example of someone dedicated to his mission. He suffered years of set-backs, yet still persevered and pursued his mission unapologetically until he became President of the USA and then he carried on to be one of the best.

I once had a friend who lived in a dirty, rented house and she and her children lived on welfare and were badly dressed. Then she began doing Bible study with some Jehovah's Witnesses who knocked at her door one day. From there she began to dress neatly, cleaned and decorated her house, got a job, attended Kingdom Hall every week, met a man and married him, bought a nice house, and totally turned her life around.

Again, her mission wasn't money-orientated, yet she did gain more money and she also completely changed her life for the better. I'd never seen her so happy.

But you can see from these example that dedicating your life to your mission can transform your life financially, emotionally and professionally.

People are drawn to those with a mission because they no longer care what anyone thinks of them. They don't want or need constructive criticism or permission to work on their mission. They only care about their mission. Other people are either inspired or intimidated by them. But either way, they want to be like them, because having a mission gives a person self-esteem which automatically makes them yield persuasive power and influence.

Don't put off getting a mission. Decide what you want to do today, and it can be anything you want:

- Financial: building a business empire
- Creative: author, musician, artist
- Religious: founding a church or joining one
- Skillful: sports, programming, acting, engineering

The only thing your mission MUST be is ongoing. It's no good saying that your mission is to build your own house, because that is a finite plan so it will end. However, saying you want to build or renovate lots of houses is OK.

Likewise, joining a church and only attending once a week on Sundays isn't enough. You need to dive deeply and completely into immersing your whole life into it. For example, Jehovah's Witnesses not only attend weekly meetings, they attend Bible study together as a congregation every week, study as a family at home once a week, go out on their ministry work together, go out on ministry work as a family, and also attend yearly and other regular meetings with other congregations, and dress, act, and live according to their Biblical beliefs. They make their religion their mission AND their life.

And that is a great example of how you should ruthlessly pursue your own mission. everything else must come second.

This doesn't mean that you should shirk your family obligations or any of your other responsibilities, but the emotional, financial, and security and wellbeing trickles down from someone who is taking care of their mission which will eventually benefit everyone.

You must understand though, that putting your mission first and working on it every day will change your life and set forces in motion like you've never seen before. THAT'S how powerful having a mission can be.

People will respect you and eventually you'll have more money, persuasive power and influence.

Naturally, there will be setbacks and challenges, and you may sometimes feel like quitting.

Others will force their negative opinions on you, through jealousy and owing to the fact that they'll feel lesser about themselves because of you, and are afraid of the success and power you'll gain.

So be ready for setbacks and jealousy, but don't let it stop you. The opinions of others are their problem, not yours.

I find that my family can be the worst when it comes to jealousy and negativity. They've never understood my desire and determination to be a writer. Neither my family nor my friends like it when I lock myself away at home day after day and night after night, writing and earning money instead of sitting in cafes drinking coffee and gossiping with them. Why would I want to do that when I'd much rather be on my own working on my mission?

Likewise, you should enjoy the satisfaction you get from working on your mission every day. A bad day working on your mission is better than a good day in a life of mediocrity and being just like everyone else.

Chapter 2

Stop being needy

This is something you can start doing immediately to transform your life. And that is, stop being needy.

You don't need the approval of others to break away from them and work on your mission.

Stop being a people-pleaser and letting others overstep your boundaries.

A needy person always seems to be looking for something that's either lacking or missing from their day-to-day life. That's how you can tell that they're needy.

Those who aren't needy don't go out of their way to hang out or talk to other people. They live a mostly private life and can usually only handle other people in small doses.

Even when people get in touch to 'do lunch' or 'come visit' they are careful with whom they spend their valuable time and have an extremely low tolerance for anyone who doesn't value their time. They understand that you can love and respect your friends and family and be willing to do just about anything for them, but that doesn't mean that you have to go out of your way to talk to or to visit them.

Not being needy attracts others to you who aren't needy either, because they're easier to get along with and aren't offended when they don't get your attention all the time.

But not being needy also makes others want to be around you and they will get upset when they don't get all your attention, yet they will be always ready to help you without hesitation.

Not being needy is so important because it will improve all areas of your life and help you –

- have more self-esteem
- improve all your relationships - romantic, friends, family, professional, etc.
- attract the right people and the right opportunities into your life

The biggest problem with being needy is that you spend your life dodging bullets instead of firing your own. You're too scared to stand up or stand out and so you spend your life reacting to whatever happens to you (dodging bullets) instead of standing up for yourself and living life on your own terms and not on everyone else's (firing bullets).

Being needy means you always need something - attention, a favour, a relationship... this repels people. And your neediness can be seen in your tone of voice, your body language and your words. It can be seen in everything about you so you can't hide it.

No one wants to be around a needy person. It's an unattractive quality.

There are certain 'tells' of neediness:

- talking a lot when trying to persuade someone to do something for you
- talking a lot when trying to persuade someone to let you do something for them
- having trouble saying 'no' to people
- apologising all the time
- scared of not being liked
- fear of losing people in your life
- giving respect to those who don't respect you
- constantly waiting for replies to messages and voicemails
- asking people to spend time with you instead of inviting them to do so
- working on other people's missions first before working on your own

Of course, there are more. If you are guilty of doing any of these things - even just one - then you are needy.

The good news is that you can stop being needy, and even better, if you've already recognised one of your needy traits in the above list, then you're already on the road to recovery.

You see, like any changes in your life, becoming un-needy goes through stages

1. Unconscious incompetence (you don't know you're needy)

2. Conscience incompetence (you know you're needy but unsure how to fix it)
3. Conscious competence (you're un-needy when you consciously think about it and stop yourself)
4. Unconscious competence (you stop being needy without even thinking about it)

Before reading this book, you were in stage 1. Now you're in stage 2. So what you need (no pun intended) is to move onto stage 3 until you automatically reach stage 4.

The question is though, how are you going to do it?

- Start withholding your interest in other people. Don't ask them to hang out with you. Instead invite them to join you somewhere that you're already going to be. That way, if they don't show, it makes no difference so you don't care whether they're there or not.
- Spend more time away from your social circle and work on your mission. Put your mission, your goals, your desires, your interests before anyone else's.
- Become a person who is hard to reach rather than a needy person who is always available. When it's harder to track you down and spend time with you, you'll be perceived as more valuable.
- Stop thinking that you're always in a popularity contest with your friends, family and colleagues.

Once you stop being available and make it harder for others to reach you, you'll have more time to devote to your mission instead of wasting time gossiping around the proverbial water cooler.

And when you do spend time in the company of other people, use the following list of 5 important things to remember so that you never lose your self-esteem and you don't slip back into your needy ways:

1. Be self confident. Like yourself. Be optimistic. Be happy with who you are, no matter where you are or who you're with. Be consistent. Don't try and be someone else. Don't talk about your problems.
2. Tell great stories. Be relevant. Never speak just to fill a silent void. Speak with conviction, say "I am sure..." not "I think, I feel, etc." Know what's going on around the world and around you.
3. Own the room when you enter it. Be authentic.
4. Make sure all conversations are about the other person.
5. Be a good listener. Be engaged. If you want to move on, make conversation brief and move on graciously.

Make your life a dictatorship, not a democracy, and you are the dictator. Dictators are never needy. They know what needs to be done and they don't need other people's opinions or permission.

Eliminating your neediness will instantly elevate your value to the world.

You'll begin to experience a peace of mind and confidence you didn't even know existed.

Being needy can chase away people and opportunities. Even if you do everything else right, being needy will sabotage your plans and your progress.

Make sure that from now on you catch yourself being needy and stop doing it.

Learn from your mistakes if you do act needy and move forward.

And next I'll tell you how to get some 'insurance' against being needy.

Chapter 3

Don't Give Away All Your Time and Money

Having money means having more power. Many people will try and tell you that the love of money is the root of all evil. Ignore them. Don't even answer. You don't have to love money, but you do need to have some.

There is a book about personal finance called, The Richest Man In Babylon, written in 1926 by George Samuel Clason. It's a very simplistic book, but it's a great guide about how to have more money without earning more.

The book is mainly a list of 7 pieces of financial advice and the first one is 'Pay Yourself First.' It doesn't put it in those exact words, but that is what it means. And this book is considered to be a must-read by top financial experts.

Paying yourself first means that the first 10% of everything you earn is yours to keep. It's yours to either save or invest. And when you invest it wisely and gain compound interest or some other return on your investment, it gives you even more money without having to work for it.

Of course you still need to pay your bills and your taxes, but always keep 10% of your net income for yourself and you'll become financially independent.

And there's one thing about doing this that is really important - never make excuses or apologies for keeping 10% of your money.

This is because financial independence is mandatory for self-esteem, having more control over your life, and commanding respect.

Another way of looking at it is, how can you achieve anything if you're always worried about money?

Paying yourself first will give you both mental and emotional toughness. It forces you to cut out the unnecessary things in your finances, especially the useless crap you buy just to impress others.

I know a guy who works from home and hardly ever spends any money. It's not that he's too mean to spend it, just that his mission is his work. Years ago he bought himself a small house, for cash. It was solid but dated.

Did he renovate it? No. Why? Because house renovations weren't important to him. He just wanted to live alone and work on his mission.

So he simply moved in, had very little furniture, set up his home office in his living room, didn't own a TV, paid someone to mow his lawn every month while all he did in the garden was lay in it on nice days and read books about his business so that he could earn more money.

He had an old car that he didn't use very much because he preferred to walk everywhere, and he chose his own working hours which were usually from early evening till the early hours of the morning. His is a simple life and he never cares what others think. And in fact, most who know him are envious of how easy his life is and how much money he has because he hardly spends anything. And he has incredible peace of mind.

Knowing that you have money saved AND that it will increase every week/month as you add 10% of your income to it, is extremely empowering.

It's also so easy to do, no matter how little you earn.

There's a saying that goes something like, 'Don't save what is left after spending, instead spend what is left after saving.'

You see, a lot of what we earn is spent on things we don't need. If you don't believe me, just look around your home. Take a real good look, and see all the things that you didn't need to buy. It's usually things like pictures hanging on the walls, unnecessary pieces of furniture, nicknacks (ornaments), and all the gadgets that you thought you 'needed' but they sit in the cupboards gathering dust.

We all do it. We spend money on unnecessary things all the time. Even if you look at your credit card debt you'll see that it accumulated from buying things you wanted, rather than things you needed.

That's why paying yourself 10% of all your income isn't hard. It just makes you curb your spending on unnecessary things.

You also need to pay yourself in time every day too. This means organising your time so that you can work on your mission.

Don't leave it as something you do in your spare time. No one has spare time. NO ONE.

We all spend our time doing something, so what you have to decide is what you're going to spend less time doing so that you can spend more time on your mission.

Your mission MUST be your priority every day.

Organise your time around your mission.

When I began my mission to be a writer, it was difficult because I had a young family and a job, so time was tight. I had to squeeze in my writing time however and whenever I could.

But I never used lack of time as an excuse. I knew I needed to organise my days so that I had time to write and submit my work (I was a freelance writer back then) AND I had to make my mission my priority so I needed to cut something out of my life. I chose to spend less time with other people.

I cut out time with family and friends so that I could work at my job, look after my own family and work on my mission. These were my priorities. And dedicating myself 100% to what I had to do helped me to not worry about trivial things like whether or not I'd hurt someone's feelings by not spending time with them anymore, because I didn't want anything to distract me.

And because my mission was my side hustle and not my main income, I managed to save 100% of my writing money until I could quit my job and stop working for someone else, which was my goal.

And you can do the same. Pay yourself 10% of every dollar you earn and spend as much time as you can on your mission. It will be hard at first but you'll adapt, and without even realising it, you'll become more productive, not just with your mission, but with everything in your life.

As an example, years ago, when I was just starting out as a writer, I used to follow a guy online called Captain Tim Gorman. He was an army captain who was married with two children and even though he worked long hours and needed to spend time with his family when he was at home, he still worked for four hours every evening on his mission, which was to earn money from niche, affiliate websites.

He worked late every night and often only managed four hours sleep, but he quickly built up his side business until he was earning more money online than he received from his army salary. He then retired from his military duties to work full-time on his online mission.

And if Tim G can do it and I can do it, and millions of others can do it, you can do it too.

Pay yourself first in money and time on your mission and you'll master money and time instead of being a slave to both.

By not paying yourself first financially and in time, you're giving away your power to your job and your creditors. They own you.

But contained within the pages of this book are 10 timeless lessons for business, relationships and life. And all you have to do is simply implement just one chapter a week and you'll have more impact, peace of mind, and more money than you ever thought possible.

And in the next chapter we're going to look at what you should do with the 10% you pay yourself.

Chapter 4

Financially Secure Your Future

This is probably the most important financial advice you'll ever need and this is because having the stability of having your own financial fund will give you more confidence, security and peace of mind than you can ever imagine.

A financial fund is money that you save very time you get paid, and you never spend it. You leave it to grow and multiply.

Putting away 10% of your income every time you get paid is extremely important. I cannot impress on you enough just how important it is.

No one else will give you the financial security that saving a huge stash of money will give you.

When we're financially insecure we can find ourselves lowering our standards and doing just about anything for money including taking on jobs for little pay, putting up with a verbally and emotionally abusive boss, and even selling our possessions for far less than they're worth.

Start your fund by saving up to at least one year's income, so that if the worst happened and you had no job or no way to earn money, you'd have a 12 month safety net so that you don't have to panic.

So if someone in your family (or even you) becomes really ill or injured, or your boss makes your working life intolerable, you can walk out, knowing that you can support yourself and your family for up to a year while you/they get better and/or you find another job.

Having a financial fund is something that's talked about by many financial advisors and they all say that saving just 10% of your income is the way to do it.

If you feel that money is so tight that you can't spare 10% to put into a savings account, do it anyway, then look at all the ways you can cut back on your spending. Have a 'no-spend' year where you only spend money on necessities like buying basic food (vegetables, rice, beans, potatoes) and cut out absolutely everything that is unnecessary like meals out, haircuts and new clothes. Just do whatever it takes because you MUST put away 10% of everything that you earn from now on.

They even say that if you saved 10% of all your income right from when you first started work in your early 20s, with compound interest and pay increases, you'd be a millionaire by the time you're in your 40s. Just think about that! Think of all the money you've wasted already.

And once your 10% goes into your savings account, never touch it. Just keep saving it year after year. If you never have to touch it, it's done it's job. Keep it in a bank account, especially a high-interest account, and it will multiply faster.

This fund will stop you being needy. You'll have no problem turning down bad opportunities. Having a financial fund makes you feel powerful knowing that you don't need someone else's job, money, business deal or pay.

And if ever something really bad happens, you'll have money for lawyers fees or cash to flee with.

Having money won't solve all your problems, but not having money creates problems.

What you need to do now is to create a 12 month fund as fast as you can.

Open a savings account and set up automatic payments so that 10% of your earning goes straight into it every time you get paid. That way you won't miss it.

Sell any of your possessions that you don't need and make sure you get a good price for them. Take on a second job if you can and put that money into the account too to create your fund as fast as possible so that you have a minimum of one year of financial security quickly.

Even though you probably don't believe it right now, you'll get more confidence from having this fund and people will be able to see it in your attitude and body language, because you no longer need their money, their job or need them.

Having a financial fund will release you from the fear of not having one.

Chapter 5

You Have No Peers

Now that you have your financial fear taken care of it's time to look at your attitude to others.

All our lives we're told that we have peers, that we're no better than everyone else, but I disagree. I don't have any peers because I'm better than them, and so are you.

You see, thinking that others are your equal can cause you problems.

For a start, if you ever feel that one of your 'peers' is doing something better than you, that can make you feel useless and miserable.

This is why you need to understand that you have no peers. Knowing this helps you to live life on your terms and only allow others in if they're good enough.

This will also stop you from always being a pawn in someone else's chess game. It's your life so you live it however you want instead of how others think you should.

Take back control of yourself and stop always caring about what others think. Never forget that your life is a dictatorship, not a democracy, so they don't get a vote on what you do.

Always giving a damn what others think causes you to put others on a pedestal because you think their opinion is more important than yours. And once you put them on a pedestal, they can only look down on you.

Even if you're financially successful and respected by others, you can lose it all by putting even one person on a pedestal, no matter how important you think they are.

Heed the Bible warning that says you should never put your trust in men (or women). And because no one is ever what they seem (even Satan was once considered an angel). No one is 100% trustworthy, so trust no one. Only trust your mission.

Putting someone on a pedestal makes you look weak, like someone to be pitied.

Only put your mission on a pedestal so that you always let it take priority.

Putting a person on a pedestal gives them your power. Even if you never say that you've placed them there, it will show in your words, your body language and your actions. You won't be able to hide it.

Always remember that others should be putting you on a pedestal while you ruthlessly pursue your mission. Doing so will elevate you in the eyes of others and make you irresistible. People will want to spend time with you. But you won't have time for them.

I'm not saying to be rotten to other people, but don't put them on a pedestal either.

Only put your mission on a pedestal.

And one of the best examples I've ever come across of someone having a mission and prioritising it, is in the Book of Proverbs in the Bible.

It's not a passage about God or Jesus, and even if you're not religious at all it's still an inspiring piece of writing, and shows you exactly how to have a mission and prioritise it AND how doing so can benefit others.

It's about being a noble wife and it clearly demonstrates how powerful having a mission can be, and also shows how others respect those with a mission. Before you read it, to help you understand a couple of the lines which mentions the city gates, in those times respected elders of the community would sit inside the gates of the city where they would make laws and decisions to help everyone who lived within the city walls.

It's the Epilogue of the last Proverb number 31, New International Version:

The Wife of Noble Character

A wife of noble character who can find?

She is worth far more than rubies.

Her husband has full confidence in her and lacks nothing of value.

She brings him good, not harm, all the days of her life.

She selects wool and flax and works with eager hands.

She is like the merchant ships, bringing her food from afar.

She gets up while it is still dark; she provides food for her family and portions for her servant girls.

She considers a field and buys it; out of her earnings she plants a vineyard.

She sets about her work vigorously, her arms are strong for her tasks.

She sees that her trading is profitable, and her lamp does not go out at night.

In her hand she holds the distaff and grasps the spindle with her fingers.

She opens her arms to the poor and extends her hands to the needy.

When it snows she has no fear for her household; for all of them are clothed in scarlet.

She makes coverings for her bed; she is clothed in fine linen and purple.

Her husband is respected at the city gate, where he takes his seat among the elders of the land.

She makes linen garments and sells them, and supplies the merchants with sashes.

She is clothed with strength and dignity; she can laugh at the days to come.

She speaks with wisdom, and faithful instruction is on her tongue.

She watches over the affairs of her household and does not eat the bread of idleness.

Her children arise and call her blessed; her husband also, and he praises her: "Many women do noble things, but you surpass them all."

END

You can see from just this short passage how having a simple mission like being a good wife can benefit the whole family and provide money, position, satisfaction and a peaceful mind.

She didn't have peers nor did she care about what others did or thought. And all because she put her mission on a pedestal and always prioritised it.

And that's what you need to do too.

Chapter 6

Remember That nice guys always finish last

There's something that most people don't get, but it's something that you really need to understand if you ever want to move forward in your life. And it's this...

The world isn't going to be fair to you just because you're fair.

It doesn't matter how much of a 'nice guy' you try to be, everyone else will just be who they are, and many will try to take advantage of those who try to be nice all the time.

I learned this lesson years ago when I'd been working as a writer for a couple of years and someone emailed me to ask for advice.

She said that she too wanted to quit her job and write for a living but she wasn't sure where to start.

So I emailed her back and explained, in detail, exactly how I started and which writing course I did.

She thanked me and said that she was going to do the course too, so I thought that was it and that she was now on her merry way to becoming a writer and I could get back to my own writing now that I'd given her my best advice - for free.

But she wasn't finished with me. She emailed me again several times, complaining that the course was wrong and that it was not the way to earn money from writing and how she was going to do it a different way because she was sure she knew how to do it better.

I responded to each of her emails and assured her that if she would just stick with the course to the end, she would earn a lot of money, and that the most important thing was to be consistent and get into the habit of writing every day.

I pleaded with her to just carry on with the course in the way it was set out and see what happened.

But nope. She just sent even more emails complaining that the course simply didn't work and what a waste of money it was (it was less than $50) because she'd been writing for weeks and had earned absolutely nothing.

So I sent her one last email and told her that she couldn't possibly know that the course didn't work because she hadn't tried it, and that doing things her own way and earning no money only proved that her way didn't work. I ended it by saying that she'd asked for my advice and I'd given it, but if she didn't want to take it then I couldn't help her.

I then blocked her email address. She had wasted so much of my time already and I wasn't prepared to give her any more. And I've never made the mistake of doing that again.

It's taken me many years to realise that being nice makes me come across as being needy.

I used to let people walk all over me because I would spend my time trying to not let anyone down even though they let me down over and over. No matter what anyone said or did, I'd smile and try to be polite.

Then one day I read a book about how to be assertive. It said that being assertive is simply standing up for what you want in a passive way, and it shouldn't be confused with being aggressive.

It was a great read and it was full of examples of different situations of when you should say no, yet I would have said yes to them all. That was when I realised what a push-over I'd been all my life.

I'd always thought that if someone asked me to do them a favour, unless I had a reason why I couldn't do it, I was obligated to say yes. I'd always believed that if someone was your friend you were obliged to help them. But according to this book, I didn't have to do anything if I didn't want to, and that once I started to say no then people would stop asking.

This was empowering information. Not only could I say no, but I didn't owe anyone an explanation.

At the time I was having a problem with a neighbour. She worked just 2 hours a day because she was on welfare and so couldn't earn much money before the welfare payments were taken off her.

But she had a sickly young daughter who she could take to work with her, but when the child was too ill, she'd ask me to babysit while she worked. As you can imagine, this put a burden on me that I didn't want, but she had no one else to turn to if I said no.

But now that I was emboldened with my new assertive attitude, the next time she asked me I said no. She asked why, so I told her I simply didn't want to and that it was unfair of her to keep asking me.

She pleaded with me and said that she needed the money but I said that if her child was so ill then she should be at home with her. And to be honest, her child never seemed THAT ill to me anyway. I think she just preferred to be with me instead of at work with her mother, or that the mother just wanted to go to work on her own.

I stood my ground that day, even though I felt like giving in. And it worked. She never asked me to look after her daughter again and she took her to work with her every day after that.

And now the way I judge things is that I always ask myself, 'What's in it for me?' And if the gain is not mine or it's something that I really don't want to do, then I say 'No thanks. I don't want to.'

It's so empowering.

And it's not too late for you to do the same.

Don't mistreat anyone or be aggressive or abusive, but do be assertive.

- Lay down strict boundaries of what you will/will not accept
- End toxic relationships and expel low-class people from your life
- Be particular about who you spend your time with
- If you're good at something, never do it for free

- Be selfish. Don't feel that you need to 'help' everyone who asks
- Stay away - far away - from anyone trying to harm you
- Don't respect anyone who doesn't respect you
- Don't put anyone on a pedestal

It's time to stop being the 'nice' person or the 'fair' person at everyone else's beck and call.

Command respect instead of pity and people will treat you differently but in a good way.

Always remember that people will treat you as badly as you allow them to.

So slay your inner 'nice guy' and stop being grateful for all the crumbs others throw you.

Nice guys always finish last because they put everyone else's needs before their own.

Stop expecting the world to be fair to you.

It's your life so you decide who is good enough to be invited into it, and who is worthy of your time, instead of being needy of being 'liked' for the nice guy you always try and be to everyone.

Chapter 7

Time is your time all the time

I first heard about the concept of time vampires from Dan Kennedy's book, No B.S. Time Management. I originally borrowed it from my local library and I got so much great information from it that I went and bought a copy of my own so that I could read it several more times.

If you've never read this book, you should because it shows you so many ways in which we waste time without even realising it, and how we let others steal our time.

And in Chapter 2 of this book is where he goes into detail about what he calls Time Vampires.

These are people who use and abuse our time, and time is our most precious commodity. It's how we use our time that determines what type of life we have and how successful we are.

Some of the time vampires you might have already met at work are:

Mr Have-you-got-a-minute

Mr Let's-have-a-meeting

Mr Trivia

When someone asks, 'Have you got a minute?' They not only want a lot more than a minute, but they demand it right now. If you tell them you don't have a minute but you'll give them 10 minutes later, they're not interested.

The person who always wants to have meetings is a real time vampire because meetings always take longer than necessary.

And people who waste time talking about trivial things should really stop talking.

But these aren't the only time vampires. There are so many different varieties.

And you'll find that as soon as you decide to pursue your mission, time vampires will rise up from everywhere.

If you want to have enough time to work on your mission, you can do so by avoiding the following types of people:

- Friends, family and colleagues who want to debate everything, especially on social media where they try and bully you if you dare have a different opinion to theirs. They want to suck you into debates that you have no interest in, debates about things that don't even matter. And the more of your time they get to waste, the more they like it.
- Small-minded people who like to waste time on small talk and gossip. Every time they see you they command your attention and waste your time talking about trivial matters until you feel exhausted.

46

- Persistent text messagers. These people waste your time by not only continually bombarding you with text messages every minute of every day, but they expect you to respond immediately. The worst of these types are the ones who will call you and demand to know why you're not responding, even though their messages are all trivia based.
- Those who are always late whenever you're supposed to meet them somewhere, or they always manage to keep you waiting in other ways. This is how they take control of your time and also control you.
- Perpetual interrupters. These are people who continually interrupt you either by calling round uninvited or calling you on the phone. And no matter what you say to them, they always think that whatever you're doing isn't as important as whatever they have to say.
- Opinionated people who insist on giving you their view about everything, whether you want to hear it or not. If you try and tell them that their opinions are wrong or that you're not interested, it only makes them worse as they insist on detailing why they're right, right, right and how wrong you are for not wanting to hear any of it.

These are just a few of the time vampires out there. Once you're aware of them you'll notice that there are many more types.

You need to be on your guard against them. The way I know that someone is a time vampire is if they're taking up too much of my time talking about things I don't really need to know about, or things that don't interest me.

Just like fictional vampires, they can only get to you if you invite them in, so never invite them into your life. Not even for a minute, because as I said before they always want to suck away much more than a minute of your time.

And on the occasions when they do get in, ignore them. Ignoring them is one of the most effective things you can do to get rid of them because time vampires hate being ignored and at the same time it gives you back your power over them.

Your ultimate goal is to eject them from your life completely.

I once had to do this to a woman who wouldn't leave me alone.

Her husband used to work with my husband. We moved away and they followed a few years later and asked for our help in finding somewhere to live and in getting to know the area.

This was fine for the first month or so, but it was biting into my writing time too much (and socialising is something I don't enjoy and find it emotionally draining) so I needed to distance myself from them as soon as possible.

I'd never met this man's wife before, yet she clung to me like a limpet and kept turning up at my house uninvited and would stay for over an hour every time, chatting on and on about nonsense.

She would tell me about other mothers she'd met when she took her son to school every morning and how they were all meeting up for coffee or lunch almost every day.

Then she'd talk at length about each of these women (none of whom I knew) and tell me all about their families and their lives. It was as though she was coming to my house immediately after being with them and imparting everything they said. And I really didn't care about any of it. The worst part was that the more she came over, the longer she stayed, until her visits were lasting up to 3 hours.

I eventually realised that she was nothing but a time vampire and I needed to get rid of her.

So the simple thing to do was not let her in. I did it by simply not answering the door. Or if it was a hot day and the door was open (which it usually was) I'd keep the screen door locked so that she had to knock and I'd say I was just about to go out, or I was busy and couldn't chat, or that I already had someone else there. I also kept saying that it would be easier if she called first because she shouldn't assume that I'd always be available.

I also started going to our local McCafe (I really like their coffee) to do my writing or working in the park or at the library so that when she rang I'd say, quite truthfully, that I wasn't at home, and I never told her where I was.

Of course, within a couple of weeks she stopped calling. And as it turned out, I enjoyed working at the cafe and the park and the library, and I found that I was much more productive that way, so I kept on doing it. So eliminating that time vampire was a win-win.

There is another type of time vampire who never seems like one , but they are.

And this one is your critics. It's those who always want to comment on what you say, what you do, or even, what you wear. Whatever it is you do, they're always there with a criticism.

These time vampires need to be shot down immediately. Listening to them is such a waste of time. I usually deal with them by asking, "Why should I care about your opinion?" To which they always respond, "I was only trying to help." To which I say, "I didn't ask for your help." To date, it shuts them down every time.

And you can do it too. Stop wasting time seeking approval and being needy for their 'likes'.

You don't need anyone's approval or opinion, especially if you didn't ask for it.

Always be on the lookout for time vampires. They're everywhere. Without realising it you probably meet several every day. You can spot them if you're paying attention. They're the ones who want to talk about trivial or unimportant things. Never anything life-changing. And they usually only talk about themselves.

They sap your energy if you let them.

Keep a watch out for them and cut them off before they take too much of your time.

Chapter 8

Ignore The Masses

If there is one thing that you need to stay away from if you want to be successful and have a great life, it's wanting to be like everyone who doesn't have a mission.

Most people who don't have a mission do nothing but simply follow the 'flock' of all the masses of sheeple. They spend their time worrying, are afraid of being different, are scared of not being accepted by the other sheeple, and needy of being liked.

They think that just because the masses of sheeple think that something is the accepted and 'right way' to do something, then anyone who dares to question them or who disagrees, is wrong. They never stop to think that just because it's the accepted 'right way' doesn't mean that it IS the right way.

So if they tell you that spending so much time on your mission is wrong, then turn the tables on these nay-sayers. Spend even more time on your mission, become successful and leave the sheeple to their own wasted lives.

Don't think that you ever need the opinion of others as to whether spending most of your time on your mission is right. Have the confidence to politely tell them that it's none of their business.

Go after your mission without apology or hesitation. Push back more and you'll have more impact in your personal and business life.

Keep people away from your mission. The more they know the more they'll use it against you.

Always keep others at least an arms distance when you're working so they can never get near your mission and interfere in something that has nothing to do with them whatsoever.

It never ceases to amaze me how sheeple get so jealous about those who have a mission. They seem unable to comprehend that you'd rather spend time on your mission than with them, even though they lead mediocre lives that are so dull and empty that they struggle to find enough time-wasting activities to fill their days.

Yet they'll still try and tell you that working on your mission is wrong.

Ignore the naysayers and those who try to force their negative and unsolicited feedback on you. Your mission is not their business and they must learn that.

When you ignore the masses and give all your time and attention to your mission, they'll get annoyed, 'offended' and often downright nasty.

But who cares?

It's your life and your mission so you don't owe them any explanation, but boy will they think you do.

Just ignore them. Not answering their demands and refusing to answer their questions will hurt them. But that's their problem.

Just remember this saying: -

'A lion never loses sleep over the opinions of sheep.'

Let them know by ignoring them and by your actions and success, that you no longer care what they think, say or do.

I cannot explain adequately enough how empowering it is to have a mission. It gives you the confidence to turn your back on the masses because you no longer need their time and attention and you won't really care if they like you or not. And funnily enough, in my experience, once everyone got used to the idea that my time now belonged to my mission and not to them, once their jealousy, confusion, annoyance and anger died down, they accepted this new way of things.

I still don't spend much time with them but that's OK because I neither need to nor want to.

Having a mission and putting it on a pedestal and ignoring the discomfort that it causes the masses of sheeple, is much more than something you do.

It enables your confidence and self-esteem to grow.

It gives you a power you never thought you could have.

Having a mission can quite literally save your life.

Chapter 9

Have patience

Without doubt, patience is the most deadly weapon you can possess.

When you're needy, it makes you impatient and that is what can trip you up.

This is especially true when it comes to impatient speaking. When you talk impatiently it makes you say things without thinking them through first. Things you later regret.

Patience takes self-discipline and without it, you'll spend your whole life regretting things you said and did.

And as the motivational speaker and author Jim Rohn said, 'We must all suffer from one of two pains: the pain of discipline or the pain of regret. The difference is discipline weighs ounces while regret weighs tons.'

So if you want to protect yourself from hasty speech and hasty actions and reactions, then you need to practice self-discipline and patience, both of which go hand in hand.

I earlier described patience as a weapon and that's because it not only protects you from being hasty, but it hurts other people when you don't react to them.

A great example of patience is watching the current Dalai Lama, Tenzin Gyatso. Not only does he move slowly, but he always hesitates for a few seconds before he speaks because he's thinking of exactly what he's going to say. This is how he uses patience to protect himself from rash movements and hasty speech.

And have you ever watched a Clint Eastwood movie? It doesn't matter if it's one of his old western movies or a more modern one like Grand Torino, he always plays a patient character.

He's always the man of few words who never seems to get flustered or agitated. And this causes others to seek him out and try and ruffle his proverbial feathers just to get a reaction from him. But he always remains patient.

Another good example of how powerful patience is, is by reading about Buddhism. The Buddhists practice Mindfulness throughout every day of their lives.

Being Mindful means only ever thinking about the present moment without letting your thoughts drag you back into the past or start worrying about the future.

They say that we can only control the present moment that we are living in so this is all we should be thinking about. Our whole attention should be on whatever we are doing.

This is what makes Buddhist monks and nuns so quiet, unhurried and patient.

Mindfulness is actually a difficult thing to master, but once achieved it can bring untold benefits which include mental rest (from too many thoughts), calmness of mind, and patience.

And no matter where you look or what stories you read, patience is always a powerful virtue. The best weapon to have.

One of the best examples of patient and mindfulness is the old Leo Tolstoy motivational story of 'The Three Questions.' It's a really clever parable, and it concerns a king who wants to find the answers to what he considers to be the three most important questions in life, and you can read it below:

The Three Questions

One day it occurred to a certain king that if he only knew the answers to three questions, he would never stray in any matter. What is the best time to do each thing? Who are the most important people to work with? What is the most important thing to do at all times? The king issued a decree throughout his kingdom announcing that whoever could answer the questions would receive a great reward. Many who read the decree made their way to the palace, each person with a different answer.

In reply to the first question, one person advised that the king make up a thorough time schedule, consecrating every hour, day, month, and year for certain tasks and then follow the schedule to the letter. Another person replied that it was impossible to plan in advance and that the king should put all vain amusements aside and remain attentive to everything in order to know what to do at what time. Someone else said that certain matters required immediate decision and could not wait for consultation, but if he wanted to know in advance what was going to happen he should consult magicians and soothsayers.

The responses to the second question also lacked accord.

One person said that the king needed to place all his trust in administrators, another urged reliance on priests and monks, while others recommended physicians. Still others put their faith in warriors.

The third question drew a similar variety of answers. Some said science was the most important pursuit. Others insisted on religion. Yet others claimed the most important thing was military skill.

The king was not pleased with any of the answers, and no reward was given. A few days later, the king went to visit a hermit who lived up on the mountain and was said to be an enlightened man. The king wished to find the hermit to ask him the three questions, though he knew the hermit never left the mountains and was known to receive only the poor, refusing to have anything to do with persons of wealth or power. So the king disguised himself as a simple peasant and ordered his attendants to wait for him at the foot of the mountain while he climbed alone to seek the hermit. Reaching the holy man's dwelling place, the king found the hermit digging a garden in front of his hut. When the hermit saw the stranger, he nodded his head in greeting and continued to dig.

The king approached him and said, "I have come here to ask your help with three questions: When is the best time to do each thing? Who are the most important people to work with? What is the most important thing to do at all times?" The hermit listened attentively but continued digging. The king said, "You must be tired. Here, let me give you a hand with that." The hermit thanked him, handed the king the spade, and then sat down on the ground to rest.

After he had dug two rows, the king stopped and turned to the hermit and repeated his three questions. The hermit still did not answer. One hour passed, then two. Finally the sun began to set behind the mountain. The king put down the spade and said to the hermit, "I came here to ask if you could answer my three questions. But if you can't give me any answer, please let me know so that I can be on my way."

The hermit lifted his head and asked the king, "Do you hear someone running over there?" The king turned his head. They both saw a man emerge from the woods. He ran wildly, pressing his hands against a bloody wound in his stomach. The man ran toward the king before falling unconscious to the ground, where he lay groaning. Opening the man's clothing, they saw that the man had received a deep gash. The king cleaned the wound thoroughly and then used his own shirt to bandage it, but the blood completely soaked it within minutes. He rinsed the shirt out and bandaged the wound a second time and continued to do so until the flow of blood had stopped.

Meanwhile, the sun had disappeared and the night air had begun to turn cold. The hermit gave the king a hand in carrying the man into the hut where they laid him down on the bed. The man closed his eyes and lay quietly. The king was worn out from the long day of climbing the mountain and digging the garden. Leaning against the doorway, he fell asleep. When he rose, the sun had already risen over the mountain. For a moment he forgot where he was and what he had come here for. He looked over to the bed and saw the wounded man also looking around him in confusion. When he saw the king he said in a faint whisper, "Please forgive me."

"But what have you done that I should forgive you?" the king asked. "You do not know me, your majesty, but I know you. I was your sworn enemy, and I had vowed to take vengeance on you, for during the last war you killed my brother and seized my property. When I learned that you were coming alone to the mountain to meet the hermit, I resolved to surprise you on your way back down to kill you. But after waiting a long time there was still no sign of you, and so I left my ambush in order to seek you out. But instead of finding you, I came across your attendants, who recognised me, giving me this wound. Luckily, I escaped and ran here. If I hadn't met you I would surely be dead by now. I had intended to kill you, but instead you saved my life! I am ashamed and grateful beyond words. If I live, I vow to be your servant for the rest of my life, and I will bid my children and grandchildren to do the same. Please grant me your forgiveness."

The king was overjoyed to see that he was so easily reconciled with a former enemy. He not only forgave the man but promised to return all the man's property and to send his own physician and servants to wait on the man until he was completely healed. After ordering his attendants to take the man home, the king returned to see the hermit. Before returning to the palace the king wanted to repeat his three questions one last time. He found the hermit sowing seeds in the earth they had dug the day before. The hermit stood up and looked at the king. "But your questions have already been answered." "How's that?" the king asked.

"Yesterday, if you had not taken pity on me and given me a hand with digging these beds, you would have been attacked by that man on your way home. Therefore the most important time was the time you were digging, the most important person was myself, and the most important pursuit was to help me. Later, when the wounded man ran up here, the most important time was the time you spent dressing his wound, for if you had not cared for him he would have died and you would have lost the chance to be reconciled with him. Likewise, he was the most important person, and the most important pursuit was taking care of his wound. Remember that there is only one important time and it is Now. The present moment is the only time over which we have dominion. The most important person is always the person with whom you are with, who is right before you, for who knows if you will have dealings with any other person in the future. The most important pursuit is whatever you need to do at that moment."

END.

See how life-changing - not to mention life-saving - mindfulness can be?

And mindfulness cannot be achieved without patience and on the flip side, you need patience in order to be able to practice mindfulness. One cannot exist without the other.

But it takes a lot of mastered discipline to acquire patience. Sometimes patience is perceived as a passive act, but we know from the Buddhist tradition that patience is self-mastery that required absolute control over our thoughts, words and deeds.

Patient people soon discover that too much action is actually inaction. Reacting impatiently to every little thing is not taking action. It's merely reacting, or, in many cases, over-reacting.

Never mistake activity for productivity.

You can't control everything, so don't even try.

Just slow down and only take control of what you can control. You can't control what happens to you, but you can control how you respond to it.

Patient people are activists waiting for the right time to act, and for the right reasons to do it in the right way.

It was former British Prime Minister Margaret Thatcher who said, 'I am extraordinarily patient, provided I get my own way in the end.' And she was always rewarded for her patience by getting exactly what she wanted.

Few people have patience, this is why it's 100-times rarer than gold and 1,000-times more valuable.

Grow it. Nurture it. Strengthen it.

Patience seeps into every part of your life and improves it:

- Reputation
- Authority
- Creativity
- Family life
- Relationships
- Friendships
- Financial wealth
- Ability to inspire others

Most importantly, it will improve your ability and capacity to pursue your mission.

Patience is like a muscle and should be exercised daily.

It will help you to progress confidently and enable you to walk away from all your enemies, haters, competitors, and naysayers, leaving them to wonder how you managed to beat them all.

And the secret is not to work on how to defeat them, but to focus on yourself and learn self-discipline and patience.

Strangely, you need patience to build self-discipline, and then you use self-discipline to practice patience. So it's easy to see how the two go naturally hand-in-hand, and are a huge stepping stone to helping you work on your mission.

Chapter 10

Persistence

In the last chapter we talked about patience and how it can help you pursue your mission while at the same time giving you the confidence to walk away from naysayers, enemies and haters. And believe me, once you start to pursue your mission, negative people will appear from everywhere and try and stop you.

So while cultivating patience will help to carry you through tough times and bad attitudes from others, persistence will push you to keep going.

Think about this... we all know that Edmund Hilary was the first person to climb to the top of Mount Everest. But did you know he did it on his third attempt? That's right. He and his team climbed that mountain again and again until they made it to the top. Without persistence they would have given up after the first try.

And the same will happen to you. Without persistence you'll remain in the foothills with all the other people living their mediocre lives, instead of reaching up to climb the mountain and rise up above the others.

Persistence is a unique mental strength and is essential to combat all obstacles that get in your way. It's also what separates successful people from all the rest.

In the business world, it's why 20% of the sales people take home 80% of commissions. Persistence drives them to keep trying and keep improving, while the other 80% give up and so only take home 20% of the sales.

When people ask me how they can be a high-earning writer like me, I tell them that they don't have to be a great writer. They just have to have the persistence to turn up and write every day so that they can out-work everyone else.

Sadly, not many want to hear the dirty 'W' word. They're looking for a quick fix that will earn them a lot of money. They don't want to be told they have to work for it. They don't understand that being a successful writer is my mission so I enjoy working on it and my persistence always pays off.

If you want to be a success with your mission you need persistence.

There is nothing that can replace it; not looks nor education nor talent nor genius nor skill. All you need is persistence and determination and you CANNOT fail. You'll also be highly productive.

Persistence is not something you're born with nor can it be inherited. The only way you can become persistent is to develop it.

But how do you do that?

To become persistent in your mission you have to want to do it really bad, so much so, that your persistence for your mission becomes automatic to the point where not being able to work on it becomes hateful, and anyone who tries to stop you better get out of your way.

And it all starts with knowing what your mission is and you do that by deciding what it REALLY is that you want to do more than anything else, and then you'll develop the persistence to pursue it and work on it as much as you possibly can.

Just don't confuse what you want to do, with what you THINK you should want to do. Listen to your heart of hearts.

Most people never admit to themselves that there is something that they've always wanted to do.

They never admit that they have a mission that they want to devote their life to. And you might feel the same way.

You may even feel that you don't deserve the right to do what you want to do, or that it's selfish to want something only for yourself.

But you'd be wrong. As long as you're not shirking your responsibilities like looking after your family, or your job, or looking after your home, then there's nothing wrong or selfish about pursuing your mission Although the naysayers and jealous people will try and tell you differently, don't listen to them. They are not you and so they cannot make decisions for you.

It's your life and you can do with it whatever you please. You are just as important as everyone else. If not MORE important.

If you don't know what your mission is (or if you think you do but you're not 100% sure), think about what it is that you truly want to do and ask yourself if you would give your life for it?

That may sound dramatic but it's not, because whatever you're doing now, you're giving your life for it. So ask yourself, was it your decision to be doing what you're currently doing? Or are you being told/led by others to do what you're doing?

Are you just following the majority of others leading a mediocre life?

Are you stuck in the foothills with everyone else instead of climbing to the top of your own mountain? If the others aren't climbing their own mountains, then that's their problem, not yours.

If you're struggling with persistence it's because your 'want' for what you're doing isn't big enough so it doesn't excite you enough.

You want something more, something bigger. Something that keeps you up late at night and every morning you wake up eager to get to work on it.

Once you know what your mission is and you begin to pursue it, your persistence will make you feel energised and motivated and make you feel great. Your reward will be fulfilment, confidence and lack of neediness.

You'll beat resistance with persistence.

You'll stop blaming others for your failures and mediocrity.

Decide what your mission in life really is, and you'll know it's the right decision because you'll want it so bad and you WILL persist in doing it.

You don't even need to know how you're going to do it, only that you want to.

And eventually, once you start working on your mission, you'll find that life will finally be what it's meant to be which will motivate you to pursue your mission with unstoppable persistence.

Afterword

I hope by reading this book you can now see how knowing what your true mission is, and pursuing it by working on it daily, can literally save your life.

There are two sides to everyone, the light side that everyone sees and the darker side lurking in the shadows. This is the side that we keep to ourselves and it holds our true opinions, goals and dreams that we don't usually discuss in public. Or to anyone.

But you cannot unleash your greatness by always hiding half of yourself.

Own your dark side for the good of all by persistently working on your mission and not allowing others to monopolise your time or crush your spirit.

Working on your mission will help you to discover the mindset needed for sheer focus and the willpower to stop hiding your shadow.

Having a mission will free you up in ways you never imagined. With your focus and drive concentrated only on your mission, you'll stop being a naysayer, a 'nice guy,' needy, and impatient.

You'll stop taking on other people's problems and all the drama that comes with it. They broke it so let them fix it, because you'll be too busy creating your dream job and living your dream life.

Once you have your mission to always turn to, you'll see the reality that in adult life, people are bullies. Adults are worse bullies than kids especially when it comes to social media, charities, protests, and even politics. If you have a different opinion to them or you don't want to support their cause, then look out!

Your mission gives you the confidence and self esteem to walk away from other people's demands.

But the caveat must be to use wisdom and ethics when applying what you've read in this book.

Remember that having a mission gives you power you never had before.

And as I told you at the beginning... just as a surgeon's knife can be used to either save a life or take a life, you too must be careful when it comes to using everything you've learned here, or you many end up in trouble or hurting someone.

And neither of us wants that to happen.

Now go and live your mission critical life filled with everything you've ever dreamed of having, including self-esteem, lack of neediness, and financial freedom.

END

I hope you enjoyed reading this book.

But even more importantly, I hope you begin to immediately put what you've learned to good use so that you can finally begin to live your life on your own terms while you pursue your mission.

You can find more life-changing and inspirational books at Cheriton House Publishing.

https://cheritonhousepublishing.com

www.ingramcontent.com/pod-product-compliance
Lightning Source LLC
Chambersburg PA
CBHW071018040426
42443CB00007B/841